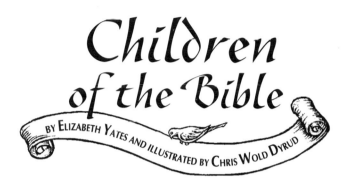

Children of the Bible

BY ELIZABETH YATES AND ILLUSTRATED BY CHRIS WOLD DYRUD

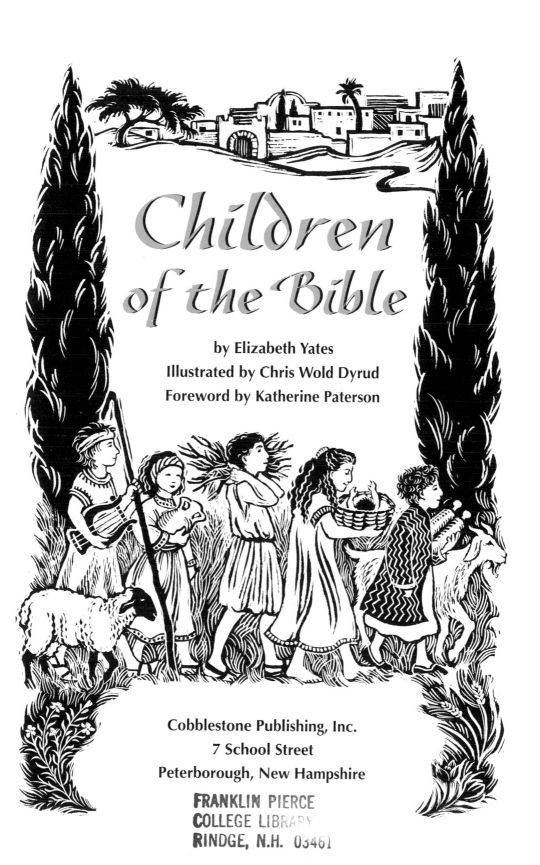

Children of the Bible

by Elizabeth Yates
Illustrated by Chris Wold Dyrud
Foreword by Katherine Paterson

Cobblestone Publishing, Inc.
7 School Street
Peterborough, New Hampshire

Manufactured in the United States of America
ISBN 0-942389-14-X

Cobblestone Publishing, Inc.
7 School Street, Peterborough, New Hampshire 03458

Library of Congress Cataloging-in-Publication Data
Yates, Elizabeth. 1905–
    Children of the Bible / by Elizabeth Yates : illustrated by Chris
Wold Dyrud.
        p.   cm.
    Reprint. Originally published: New York : Aladdin Books, 1950.
    Summary: A collection of familiar stories about children from both
the Old and New Testament.
    ISBN 0-942389-14-X (pbk.)
    1. Children in the Bible—Juvenile literature. 2. Children-
-Biblical teaching—Juvenile literature.   [1. Children in the
Bible. 2. Bible stories.]   I. Dyrud, Chris Wold, ill.   II. Title.
BS576.Y3   1996
220.9'2—dc20   96-10682
                                                       CIP
                                                       AC

Contents

Nearly fifty years since *Children of the Bible* was first published, Cobblestone Publishing is excited to issue a new edition of the classic, with its wonderful stories for children of
all ages.

In order to give the book a fresh look, we asked artist
Chris Wold Dyrud to lend her magical hand to the cover
and story illustrations and Coni Porter, designer of several of
our books, to combine the drawings and stories in a simple
flowing layout.

Elizabeth Yates, who was extremely eager to introduce
her stories to a new audience, adds a warm welcome and
writer Katherine Paterson reflects on the importance of the
stories and the joy in sharing them.

We hope you treasure these timeless stories and keep
them alive for many years to come.

The Editors

Foreword

*I*n bringing out this edition of Elizabeth Yates' classic, *Children of the Bible*, Cobblestone Publishing is giving a new generation of children an added opportunity to become acquainted with stories loved by children since those stories were first told in Hebrew, Aramaic, and Greek.

Elizabeth Yates' graceful rendering of the stories is close to the most beautiful of English translations, the Authorized King James Version of 1611, which, along with the plays of William Shakespeare, definitively shaped the English language. Like all children raised in pious Protestant homes fifty years ago, I grew up reading the King James Bible. There were many times when I found its archaic expressions baffling, but the music of its poetry and prose gave me an ear for the beauty of the language that helps explain, I feel sure, why I became a writer.

The language is so battered and abused today that I wondered as I read this book if its language would seem almost a foreign tongue to children raised on the corrupted jargon of television. I think, though, that if children hear them read aloud, these Biblical stories, like the classic tales of Beatrix Potter or A. A. Milne, will delight them and satisfy the hunger for beauty that all of us share.

These stories have been written simply, with the expectation that children would read them for themselves. It is my hope, however, that long before children are able to read, their parents will have read the stories aloud—indeed, reread them so often that when children pick up the book to read it for themselves the stories will ring in their minds like a well-loved melody.

In her wonderful book *Memories of God* (Abingdon Press, 1995), Biblical and patristic scholar Roberta Bondi recalls the great comfort she received as a child, reading about the children of the Bible. Stories gave her something to hold on to when the doctrines of her elders seemed incomprehensible or even frightening.

Elizabeth Yates' book made these stories immediately accessible to children of an earlier generation. In this new edition, they are once again available for children to enjoy—in the deepest sense of that word.

Can these retellings compete with the loud, insistent noises of the media? I dare to think they can—that is, if parents will take the time to read them aloud. What more could any child want than to sit on a loving lap and hear a quiet voice read stories of other children whom God has loved and cared for? This experience, dearly remembered, has given many of us strength. As we've grown older, we've gone back again and again to take comfort and instruction from the Bible because its stories were first given to us when we were young.

Katherine Paterson, Barre, Vermont, 1996

Preface

The Bible is a big book and a very old book, going far back in time. With its wide sweep of history, of laws and customs and great happenings, there are many stories of men and women, and of the children who were part of their lives.

Here are some of the children from families in the Bible—Isaac with his question that rings down through the ages, "But where is the lamb for a burnt offering?"; David, who was ready for the challenge that had daunted many skilled men of war; the little serving maid who had to share the good news she had heard; the boy with the loaves and fishes who gave what he had, and in so doing opened the way for a miracle.

Through the long years come the stories, up to the time of Jesus, who took a child in his arms and said to the people standing near, "In heaven their angels do always behold the face of my Father." (Matthew 18:10)

In the early days, before books became widespread, the Bible was likely the only book in a house, and families turned to it often to enrich their lives and light their ways. It was a treasured possession, and it became an important part of the history of the family as the names and dates of family members' births, marriages, deaths, and other significant events were recorded in it as they happened.

This book was first published almost fifty years ago, and the children who read it then now have children of their own, even grandchildren. It comes again, in a new dress, for their children to read and wonder about; and so the family widens.

Elizabeth Yates, Concord, New Hampshire, 1996

*J*esus and his disciples left Galilee and journeyed beyond the Jordan along the coasts of Judaea. Great numbers of people followed them, listening eagerly to the words the Master spoke. Many among them were in need of healing and Jesus healed them all. Some of the people brought their children to Jesus, wanting to have the Master put his hands on them.

The disciples spoke sharply to the people as they crowded up with babies in their arms and little ones barely able to walk holding on to their mothers' skirts, but Jesus said to them all, "Suffer little children, and forbid them not, to come unto me: for of such is the kingdom of heaven."

Then he laid his hands on them one after another—dark smooth heads and golden curls, babes in arms, boys and girls.

None was too small to receive a blessing, and none was too far back on the fringes of the crowd to go unseen by Jesus. One by one, after he had blessed the children, the parents returned to their homes. Then Jesus and his followers went on their way.

from MATTHEW, *chapter 19*

David: The Boy

Saul was king in Israel but, because of his rebellious ways, Samuel was sent by the Lord to find another king. He went to the home of Jesse, in Bethlehem, for the Lord had told Samuel that among the sons of Jesse was one who would be a ruler in Israel.

One after another the seven sons of Jesse stood before Samuel, but Samuel shook his head at each one knowing he had not yet seen the chosen of the Lord.

"Are here all thy children?" Samuel asked.

"There remaineth yet the youngest," Jesse answered, "and behold, he keepeth the sheep."

"Send and fetch him," Samuel said, "for we will not sit down till he come hither."

So Jesse called for David and brought him in. David was a strong and ruddy boy with fine eyes and a handsome face. As soon as Samuel saw him he heard the voice of the Lord saying, "Arise, anoint him: for this is he."

Samuel took the horn of oil and poured it on David's head as he stood in the midst of his brothers. Then the spirit of the Lord came upon David from that day forward. But it was not time yet for David to rule in Israel so he continued taking care of his father's sheep.

Saul was often so troubled in his mind that he could find neither peace in the day nor rest at night. His servants thought that if someone could be found who would come to him and play to him on a harp it might soothe him and make him well. They told him this and Saul asked them to find such a man for him. One of them remembered that he had seen the youngest son of Jesse, the Bethlehemite, playing skillfully on a harp. So Saul had messengers sent to Jesse asking that David might come to him.

David was with the sheep when the messengers arrived, but Jesse sent for him. Then he loaded an ass with gifts for Saul and told David to present himself before the king. Before David left, Jesse made sure that the boy had slung his harp over his shoulder.

As soon as Saul saw David, he loved the boy greatly and he appointed him to be his armor bearer. He sent a message to Jesse saying, "Let David, I pray thee, stand before me; for he hath found favor in my sight."

Saul loved, too, the sound of David's playing and whenever he was troubled in his mind or could not sleep he would ask David to play to him. David, running his hands over the harp strings, would pluck out melodies, sometimes adding to them words he had thought of when alone in the hills with his father's sheep. Saul, listening, felt refreshed and all that troubled him went from his mind and he knew what it was to be at peace.

from I SAMUEL, *chapter 16*

David: The Young Warrior

Some time later, enemies pressed down upon Israel. Saul and his armies camped in the valley of Elah, ready to do battle, when from out of the camp of the enemy came a champion to challenge them. Goliath was a powerful man, some ten feet tall, wearing a helmet of brass and a heavy coat of mail. He had greaves of brass on his legs, a javelin between his shoulders, and he carried a spear with a large iron point whose shaft was like a weaver's beam. A shield bearer went before him as he came out of his camp and challenged the Israelites.

"Why are ye come out to set your battle in array?" he shouted. "Am not I a Philistine, and ye servants to Saul? Choose you a man for you, and let him come to me. If he be able to fight with me, and to kill me, then will we be your servants. But if I prevail against him, and kill him, then shall ye be our servants, and serve us."

No one in all the camp of Israel rose to answer Goliath, so the challenger cried out again, "I defy the armies of Israel this day. Give me a man, that we may fight together."

Saul and all Israel, listening to the words of the Philistine, were dismayed and greatly afraid. For forty days, in the morning and in the evening, they heard Goliath issue his challenge, but no man among them rose to accept it.

David's three eldest brothers were with the armies of Saul that were camped in the valley of Elah, but David had returned to Bethlehem to care for his father's sheep.

Jesse called him one day and said, "Take now for thy brethren an ephah* of this parched corn, and these ten loaves, and run to the camp to thy brethren. Carry these ten cheeses unto the captain of their thousand, and look how thy brethren fare, and take their pledge." For Jesse was eager to have some assurance of the well-being of his sons.

David left his sheep with a keeper and rising early the next morning did as his father had commanded him. He came to the intrenchment just as the army was going forth to battle, raising their battle cry. David left his supplies in care of a keeper and ran forward to the battle line to greet his brothers. He talked with them quickly, giving them Jesse's messages and asking them about themselves so he could bear news home to their father. As they talked together, the champion of the Philistines, Goliath of Gath, came forward and issued his challenge.

"I defy the armies of Israel this day; give me a man, that we may fight together."

The Israelites had heard the challenge so often that they paid little heed to it, but it was the first time David had heard it. Listening to Goliath, David saw to his dismay the armies of Israel that had been forming their ranks turn and flee.

David asked about Goliath so he might be able to inform his father when he returned to Bethlehem. The men of Israel crowded around the boy to tell him of the challenger.

"What shall be done to the man that killeth this Philistine and taketh away the reproach from Israel?" David asked, "For who is this Philistine, that he should defy the armies of the living God?"

The men crowding around David told him of the riches that such a man would have and that Saul would even give him his daughter for a wife, and that the man's house would be made free in Israel.

David's eyes were shining at all he heard. There were many more questions on his tongue to ask but his eldest brother who was angered at the sight of the boy talking with the soldiers came up to him.

"Why camest thou down

*Ephah: a Hebrew measure—a little over a bushel

hither?" he asked, "And with whom hast thou left those few sheep in the wilderness? I know thy pride, and the naughtiness of thine heart. Thou art come down that thou mightest see the battle."

"What have I now done?" David said. "Is there not a cause?"

David went on talking with the soldiers and soon even the skilled men of war realized that here was someone ready to accept Goliath's challenge. So they went and told Saul and Saul sent for David.

When the boy appeared in the presence of the king, he bowed. Then standing straight and hold-ing his head high, he said to Saul, "Let no man's heart fail because of him. Thy servant will go and fight with this Philistine."

"Thou art not able to go against this Philistine to fight with him," Saul said reprovingly. "Thou art but a youth, and he a man of war from his youth."

David looked earnestly at Saul. "Thy servant kept his father's sheep," David said, "and there came a lion, and a bear, and took a lamb out of the flock. I went out after him, and smote him, and delivered it out of his mouth. And when he arose against me, I caught him by his beard, and smote him, and slew him. Thy servant slew both the lion and the bear. And this Philistine shall be as one of them, seeing he hath defied the armies of the living God."

Saul was silent, but David seeing that he had almost persuaded him said, "The Lord that delivered me out of the paw of the lion, and out of the paw of the bear, he will deliver me out of the hand of this Philistine."

"Go, and the Lord be with thee," Saul said. Then he called for his armor and put it on David—a helmet of brass on his head and a coat of mail, and he gave David his sword telling him to gird it on.

David tried to walk in the armor, but he found that it was so heavy and unwieldy that he could take scarcely one step.

"I cannot go with these," David said, "for I have not proved them."

He took them off and returned them to Saul. Then he went from the king's presence clothed as he was when he had arrived in his shepherd's clothes, with a staff in his hand and a leather bag at his belt. But he fingered his sling as he went out, testing it between his fingers.

After leaving Saul, David went to the brook that flowed through the valley of Elah and from it he chose five smooth stones which he put in his leather bag. Then he went confidently into the plain to meet the Philistine.

When Goliath saw that someone from the Israelites' camp had accepted his challenge, he left his own ranks and began to make his approach, the bearer of his shield walking directly in front of him. But when he saw that his contender was no more than a boy swinging a staff in his hand, Goliath called to him disdainfully.

"Am I a dog," he growled, "that thou comest to me with staves?"

David walked steadily on, without answering.

"Come to me," the Philistine laughed scornfully, "and I will give thy flesh unto the fowls of the air, and to the beasts of the field."

David stopped a few paces from Goliath and looked up into the face of the man towering before him. "Thou comest to me with a sword, and with a spear, and with a shield," the boy said, "but I come to thee in the name of the Lord of hosts, the God of the armies of Israel, whom thou hast defied.

"This day will the Lord deliver thee into mine hand. ...And all this assembly shall know that the Lord saveth not with sword and spear; for the battle is the Lord's, and he will give you into our hands."

Goliath knew then that his challenge had been accepted and he came forward to meet David, but so heavily and ponderously that the earth shook with his tread.

David ran to meet Goliath, as light on his feet as one of his own lambs. Putting his hand into his bag, David took out one of the smooth stones and placed it in his sling. Then with all his force and with good aim he slang it. The stone struck Goliath in the forehead. With a thud that echoed through the Vale of Elah, the man who had challenged the armies of Israel sank to the earth.

When the Philistines saw that their champion was dead they cried out in dismay. But a mighty shout of triumph went up from the armies of Israel. For they saw that the man who had challenged them had been slain, and not by any great power but by a boy with a sling and a stone who carried no sword in his hand.

from I SAMUEL, *chapter 17*

The Child Samuel

*I*n a town among the hills of Ephraim lived a man named Elkanah. Hannah, his wife, had no children, but she longed for a son and prayed earnestly for one.

Once a year, all the people in the countryside went up to the temple that was at Shiloh to worship and offer sacrifices. Year after year, when Hannah went to the temple with Elkanah she offered her prayers for a son. One day, as she prayed, she made a promise to God that if God would give her a son she would give him to the Lord to serve him all the days of his life.

Before a year had gone by, a son was born to Hannah and she called his name Samuel, saying, "Because I have asked him of the Lord."

When Samuel was three years old, Hannah brought him to the temple at Shiloh. As she presented him to Eli, the priest, she said, "For this child I prayed; and the Lord gave me what I asked of him. Therefore I have lent him to the Lord. As long as he lives he shall be lent to the Lord."

So Samuel remained at Shiloh and Eli taught him how to minister to the Lord in the temple.

Every year Hannah came to see her son. She brought with her a little coat which she had made herself and which Samuel wore over his tunic. Samuel grew and his mother was proud of him. Eli was pleased with the way he carried out his tasks, opening the doors for the morning service and keeping oil in the lamps.

Eli had two sons, but they were not good as their father was and Eli scolded them often for their evil deeds. But Eli was old and his eyes were failing and his sons paid no attention to anything he said.

One night, while the lamp was still burning in the temple after Samuel had gone to his bed to sleep, the Lord called to him.

The boy sat up in bed and thinking that Eli had called him answered, "Here I am," and ran

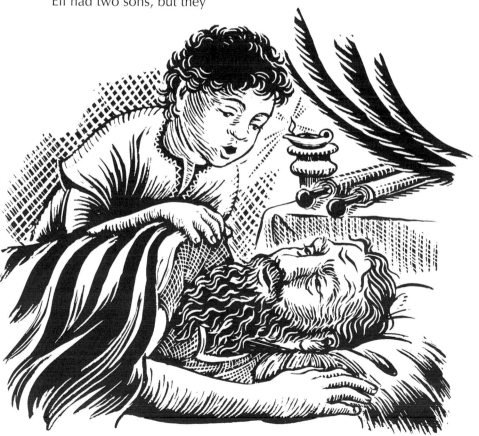

quickly to him. "Here am I," he said, "Did you call me?"

Eli said, "I called not. Lie down again."

So Samuel went back to his bed, but before he had fallen asleep the Lord called him again.

"Samuel."

Samuel rose and went to Eli. "Here am I," he said, "for you did call me."

"I called not, my son," Eli answered. "Lie down again."

Samuel went back to his bed, puzzled at the voice he had heard that was not Eli's, for never before had Samuel heard the Lord, only the voice of Eli in the temple calling him to duty or devotion.

The Lord called Samuel again the third time and for the third time the boy arose and went to Eli saying, "Here am I; for you did call me."

Then Eli knew that it was the Lord who had called the child and he said to him, "Go, lie down: and it shall be, if he call thee, that thou shalt say, Speak, Lord; for thy servant heareth."

Samuel went and lay down again and again the Lord came and stood and called, "Samuel, Samuel."

The boy answered, "Speak; for thy servant heareth."

The Lord spoke and in his words he revealed to Samuel the doom that would follow the house of Eli because of the evil ways of Eli's sons.

Samuel lay wide awake until morning, thinking of all that he had heard. When the time came for him to open the doors of the house of the Lord, he fulfilled his duty but he feared to tell Eli of the vision that had come to him in the night. Samuel loved Eli and did not want to hurt him.

"Samuel, my son," Eli called.

"Here am I," Samuel answered.

Then Eli asked him what the Lord had said to him.

And Samuel told him all, hiding nothing from him.

"It is the Lord," Eli said, quietly and humbly. "Let him do what seemeth him good."

For the old man knew as he looked at the boy that this was the one who would carry on the priesthood.

So Samuel grew and the Lord was with him and all Israel knew that Samuel was to become a prophet to the Lord.

from I SAMUEL, chapters 1, 2, 3

Abraham and Ishmael

Abraham was a man rich in lands and cattle. He was a faithful follower of the Lord and he had been told by God that he would be the founder of the Hebrew nation. But he was growing old and still he and his wife Sarah had no son. Sarah had an Egyptian handmaid, whose name was Hagar, and one day she gave Hagar to Abraham to be his wife. In time, Hagar bore a son to Abraham and the boy was called Ishmael which means "whom God hears."

When Ishmael was a young boy, God appeared again to Abraham and told him that Sarah also would have a son and that her son would be very great, numbering kings among his descendants.

This made Abraham happy for no matter how much he loved Ishmael he knew that the son of a bondwoman could never be equal to the son of a free woman.

At the set time of which God had spoken, Sarah bore a son to Abraham and his name was called Isaac. Isaac means "laughter" and this was the name by which God had said the boy should be called. There was great rejoicing in the household of Abraham. Sarah was proud of her son. Looking at him she would say, "God hath made me to laugh, so that all that hear will laugh with me."

The child grew and on the day he was weaned Abraham made a feast. The two boys, Isaac and Ishmael, played together while the people feasted. Seeing them, Abraham smiled in his pleasure at them but Sarah felt angry and disturbed. She wanted her son Isaac to have all of his father's affection and wealth. She turned to Abraham and spoke sharply.

"Cast out this bondwoman and her son: for the son of the bondwoman shall not be heir with my son, even with Isaac."

Abraham was saddened by Sarah's request, for he loved his son Ishmael only a little less than Isaac, and he loved Ishmael's mother Hagar. Abraham did not know what to do until he heard the voice of God and then he felt comforted.

For God told him to do as Sarah asked, but not to feel badly, for both Ishmael and Isaac would be the leaders of great nations.

Abraham rose early the next morning and called Hagar and Ishmael to him. He told them that they must go away and he gave them a loaf of bread and a bottle of water. Then he bade them farewell. It was not easy for him to part with them for he loved them dearly. But in doing so hard a thing he was strengthened by the promise he had received from God and he knew that wherever Hagar and Ishmael went he could trust God to care for them.

Hagar wandered far and wide in the wilderness of Beer-sheba. Ishmael held her hand tightly. When he grew tired and began to stumble over the stones, Hagar pulled him along after her. In her fear and sorrow, she knew only that they must keep going. Yet where they were going she did not know. Hagar lost her way and then she lost her hope of finding it again. Tired and thirsty, they had been drinking from the bottle of water all through the long hot day. Ishmael's lips were parched and the sun had burned his skin, but when Hagar put the bottle to his lips he shook his head. There was no water in it to quench his thirst or refresh him.

Hagar, in despair, thought there was nothing but death for her child, and yet she felt she could not bear to see him die. She placed him under a shrub as a small protection from the sun and she went and sat at a distance from him. His cries rang in her ears and to escape them she went away from him

as far as an arrow could be shot from a bow, but still she heard his crying.

"Let me not see the death of the child," she said.

In her weary hopelessness, she wept aloud, while the child lying under the desert shrub cried piteously.

God heard the voice of Ishmael and out of heaven the angel of God called to Hagar and said, "What aileth thee, Hagar? Fear not; for God hath heard the voice of the lad where he is. Arise, lift up the lad, and hold him in thine hand; for I will make him a great nation."

Then God opened Hagar's eyes that had been blinded by her own sorrow and she saw that there was a well of water near to the place where she had been sitting. She filled the empty bottle with water and went hastily to Ishmael. Lifting him up, she put the water to his lips

and he drank long and thirstily. She held him in her arms until they both felt strengthened and ready to go on their way.

The sun set and in the cool evening light they resumed their journey. In a little while they saw before them a cluster of houses, trees to give shade, and a well from which water could be drawn. They were received kindly by the villagers and there they dwelt for many years.

Ishmael grew tall, strong of arm and swift of foot. He became an archer, and none of all those who dwelt in the wilderness of Paran could handle a bow with greater skill. And God was with Ishmael in all that he did, wherever he went. And God kept his promise and Ishmael did become the leader of his people.

from GENESIS, *chapters 16, 17, 21*

Abraham and Isaac

Abraham talked with God freely, and gladly did all that God asked him to do. His faith in God was so great that it stood the test of many trials. But it was to be tested again when he was called upon to prove that he loved God more than he loved his son Isaac.

One day God called Abraham by his name.

"Behold, here I am," Abraham answered.

"Take now thy son, thine only son Isaac, whom thou lovest," God said, "and get thee into the land of Moriah. Offer him there for a burnt offering upon one of the mountains which I will tell thee of."

Early the next morning Abraham rose and saddled his ass. Then he called two of his young men and Isaac his son and told them that they were to make a journey into the wilderness that he might offer a sacrifice to the Lord. Together they cut wood for the burnt offering and bound it into bundles to be carried. Then they provided themselves with food and drink and started off on their journey.

For three days they traveled

into the wilderness. On the morning of the third day Abraham saw in the distance before him the hill of which the Lord had spoken. There was a sanctuary there at which sacrifice of men's most cherished possessions was sometimes made.

Abraham said to the two young men, "Abide ye here with the ass. I and the lad will go yonder and worship, and come again to you."

Abraham took the wood for the burnt offering from the back of the ass and placed it on Isaac's shoulders. Then he took the fire in his hand and a knife,

and together they went toward the mountain of the Lord.

"My father," said Isaac.

"Here am I, my son."

"Behold the fire and the wood. But where is the lamb for a burnt offering?"

"My son," Abraham answered, "God will provide Himself a lamb for a burnt offering."

So they went on their way, Isaac trusting his father as Abraham trusted the Lord.

When they came to the place of which God had told Abraham, Abraham built an altar there, setting stone upon stone carefully before he laid the wood in order on the top. Then he took the rope that had bound the wood and with it he bound his son Isaac, at his hands and at his feet. When all was in readiness, he placed Isaac on the altar upon the wood.

Isaac watched his father in all that he did, submitting to him though his eyes were large with wondering and his mind was full of the questions he dared not ask in the silence of the holy place that was the Lord's. But when Abraham took the knife and stretched his hand high above his son, Isaac shut his eyes in sudden fear.

"Abraham, Abraham," the angel of the Lord called out of heaven.

"Here I am," answered Abraham.

"Lay not thine hand upon the lad," he said, "neither do thou anything unto him: for now I know that thou fearest God, seeing thou hast not withheld thy son, thine only son from Me."

Abraham raised his eyes and looked around him and in a thicket close by he saw a ram caught by its horns. Then he unbound Isaac and lifted him off the wood on the altar and in the boy's place he put the ram, offering it as a burnt offering instead of his son.

Abraham called the name of the place Jehovah-jireh, and when Isaac asked what the name meant Abraham said, "In the mount of the Lord it shall be seen."

The angel of the Lord called out of heaven a second time, telling Abraham that because he had been willing to do as the Lord demanded and had even been willing to sacrifice the son he loved so dearly the Lord would bless him and make him the founder of a people so numerous that they would be "as the stars of the heaven, and as the sand which is upon the seashore"—all these nations would be blessed because he had obeyed God's voice.

Then Isaac and his father walked together down the hill of the Lord to the place where the young men and the ass were waiting for them. Then they all went back to Beer-sheba.

from GENESIS, *chapter 22*

The Two Sons of Joseph

During the time that Joseph was living in Egypt, two sons were born to him and his wife. The elder was called Manasseh and the younger Ephraim.

Joseph's brothers and his father Jacob came to live in Egypt during the seven years of famine in their own country, and there was great rejoicing among the twelve brothers and their father when they were at last together again. Jacob was, by then, a very old man and he was eager to see his grandsons, Manasseh and Ephraim, that he might give them his blessing before he died.

One day a messenger came to Joseph saying, "Behold, thy father is sick."

Joseph took his two sons and hastened to the place where his father lived. As he went, he told the little boys again how it had been said that the Lord would deal kindly with Abraham, Isaac and Jacob, the patriarchs of Israel, whose children would be as many as the stars in the sky or the sands of the sea. Listening to him, Manasseh and Ephraim felt a great sense of importance as they walked beside their father to call on their grandfather.

When they arrived at the house, Jacob was told that his son had come to see him. Weak as Jacob was, he summoned what strength he had to greet Joseph and then he told him of the goodness that God had promised to him and to his descendants.

"Now thy two sons, Ephraim and Manasseh, which were born unto thee in the land of Egypt are mine," Jacob said, and in so saying he adopted them into his family as if they had been his own sons.

Joseph bowed in acknowledgment of the honor his father had paid him.

Jacob could not see clearly enough to distinguish the two small figures standing beside Joseph so he said, "Who are these?"

"They are my sons," Joseph answered, "whom God hath given me in this place."

"Bring them, I pray thee, unto me," Jacob said, "and I will bless them."

Joseph brought the boys to his father. The old man took them up on his knees and putting his arms around each one in turn, kissed them tenderly.

"I had not thought to see thy face," Jacob said, "and, lo, God hath showed me also thy children."

Joseph then took the two boys from their grandfather's lap and bowed on his face to the ground in reverence to his father. After that he stood the children close to their grandfather. Joseph's right hand was in Ephraim's and he placed him by Jacob's left hand; Manasseh, who was the older and should have the greater blessing, he placed at Jacob's right hand.

But Jacob stretched out his right hand and laid it on Ephraim's head and his left hand he placed upon Manasseh, doing what he did intentionally.

Jacob blessed Joseph first and then he said, "God, before whom my fathers Abraham and Isaac did walk, the God which fed me all my life long unto this day . . . bless the lads. . . ."

It displeased Joseph to see that his father had placed his right hand on the younger boy so he reached out to remove his father's hand, saying hastily, "Not so, my father, for this is the firstborn; put thy right hand upon his head." And Joseph moved Manasseh closer to Jacob.

Jacob refused to do anything different from what he had done. "I know it, my son," he said. "I know it. He also shall become a people, and he also shall be great; but truly his younger brother shall be greater than he."

So it was that when Jacob blessed the two sons of Joseph he set the younger above the elder, though he blessed them both.

from GENESIS, *chapter 48*

≫ *32* ≪

The Baby Moses

The Israelites lived in Egypt many years and became so numerous that the Egyptians feared them and thought they must find some way to reduce their numbers. The Egyptians put taskmasters over them and afflicted them with heavy burdens. They made their lives bitter with hard bondage. But still the Israelites multiplied. At last the Pharaoh issued an order against them. This order was a crushing one.

"Every son that is born ye shall cast into the river, and every daughter ye shall save alive."

This was a cruel order. It caused much grief and sorrow among the Hebrew people and for a time there were no boy children growing up in any of their homes.

The river wound its way through all the length of the land of Egypt. Along its banks tall reeds and flags grew abundantly and on its waters fragrant flowers blossomed. People had built their homes near the fertile land along the river, and by its banks the Pharaoh had a palace.

One day a son was born to a man and woman of the house of Levi who lived near the great river. The boy was such a fine baby, strong of limb and with winning ways, that his mother hid him for three months, telling no one of her son and letting none of her neighbors see him. Only Miriam, the baby's sister, played with him and helped her mother care for him.

As the baby grew and his laughter or crying could be heard beyond the walls of the

ance to God as she knew she could do.

house where the Hebrew family lived, the mother realized that soon she could no longer hide the child. When his presence was discovered, she would be severely punished because she had disobeyed the law of the Pharaoh. And she would not be the only one to be punished; her husband and her daughter Miriam would suffer with her. She decided to give the child to the river as the Pharaoh had ordered, but to trust his deliverance to God as she knew she could do.

She gathered reeds from the river bank and wove them together to make a small boat. She called it an ark, for she made it strong enough to hold the child safely and to shelter him from harm. She daubed the ark with slime and with pitch so that it would be watertight and in it she made a bed of soft linen. Then she held the little boy to her and kissed him fondly before she put him in the ark and closed the lid over him. When the child had gone to

sleep inside the ark, she took the little boat down to the river's brink and placed it among the flags growing at the edge of the water.

Miriam had helped her mother in all that she did, but she did not return to the house with her mother. Instead, she remained at a little distance from the river to see what would happen to her brother. Pretending to be playing by herself, Miriam's ears were sharp for any sound of crying from the baby. Her eyes were watchful for anyone who might come to the river and discover the little boat floating on its waters.

After a while, Miriam saw the daughter of Pharaoh coming down to the river to bathe. Her maidens walked with her along the water's edge. They were laughing and talking together, but their merriment ceased suddenly.

"What is that?" the daughter of Pharaoh said as she saw what seemed like a woven basket caught among the flags. Then she turned to one of her maids. "Go and fetch it for me," she commanded.

The maid waded into the water to fetch the ark and picking it up she carried it back to her mistress. Miriam, who was standing at a distance, moved nearer so she might see what would happen when the contents of the basket were discovered.

"Shall I open it?" the maid asked.

But the daughter of Pharaoh

said that she would open it herself.

She knelt down by the basket and lifted the latch that held the lid in place. When she removed the lid she saw the child. The baby, wakened by the sound and movement and dazzled by the sudden light, began to cry.

The daughter of Pharaoh picked him up and held him to her. "This is one of the Hebrews' children," she said, and her heart melted with pity as she saw his fine dark eyes and hair, his pink cheeks and beautiful little hands, for she knew the fate that awaited all the boy babies born in Hebrew homes.

Miriam, who had been drawing nearer all the time, approached Pharaoh's daughter and said eagerly, "Shall I go and call to thee a nurse of the Hebrew women, that she may nurse the child for thee?"

Pharaoh's daughter said to her, "Go."

The little girl ran swiftly until she got to her own home, and then she told her mother all that had happened.

"Come," she said, seizing her mother's hand, "for the daughter of Pharaoh would have someone to nurse the child for her."

When they returned, Miriam and her mother stood quietly before the daughter of Pharaoh who, with her maidens, was playing with the child. The boy was laughing and waving his hands in glee, and it was all that his mother could do to keep from embracing him so glad was she to know that he was safe.

"You sent for me, O daughter of Pharaoh," the Hebrew woman said meekly.

"Take this child away, and nurse it for me," the daughter of Pharaoh said, "and I will give thee thy wages."

The baby's mother took him in her arms and carried him back to her home. She was happy that she could care for her son for a while longer, teaching him that faith in God was an Israelite's birthright and telling him of the promises God had made to his nation.

Later on, when the baby's mother brought him to the palace, Pharaoh's daughter adopted him as her own son, calling his name Moses.

"Because I drew him out of the water," she said, as she gave to the Hebrew woman the money she had promised to pay her.

from EXODUS, *chapters 1 and 2*

Elijah and the Widow's Son

There was a drought in the land of Israel and for a long time neither dew nor rain fell. The fields could not yield a harvest and all the brooks dried up. Even the brook Cherith, beside which the prophet Elijah had been dwelling, went dry. Elijah heard the word of the Lord telling him what to do.

"Arise, get thee to Zarephath," God said, "and dwell there. Behold, I have commanded a widow woman there to sustain thee."

So Elijah went to the city. Approaching it, he saw a widow woman gathering sticks. He called to her and asked her to bring him a drink of water.

As she went to get it, he called to her again and asked her to bring him a piece of bread.

She turned to him, wondering who this man was that did not seem to know there was famine in the land.

"As the Lord thy God liveth," she said, "I have not a cake, but a handful of meal in a barrel, and a little oil in a cruse. Behold, I am gathering two sticks, that I may go in and dress it for me and my son, that we may eat it and die."

"Fear not," Elijah said to her. "Go and do as thou hast said. But make me thereof a little cake first, and bring it unto me, and after make for thee and for thy son. For thus saith the Lord God of Israel, 'The barrel of meal shall not waste, neither shall the cruse of oil fail, until the day that the Lord sendeth rain upon the earth.'"

Marveling at Elijah's words but willing to believe them, the woman went to her home and did all that Elijah asked her to do. Furthermore, she prepared a room for Elijah in her house. All the time that the prophet remained in Zarephath, he stayed at the home of the widow woman and her son, and all the time the three of them ate in plenty. The word that Elijah had spoken was true, for the barrel of meal was never empty and neither did the cruse of oil fail.

And then, one day, the woman's son fell sick. So severe was his sickness that there was no breath at all left in him. In her sorrow, the woman chided Elijah for she thought she must have done some great wrong to have such evil come to her as the death of her son.

"Give me thy son," Elijah said.

Gently he took the child from the woman's arms, and carried him up the stairs to the little room that had been given to him. He laid him on the bed and prayed to God. Then he stretched himself upon the child, once, twice, three times in all, and he never ceased praying.

"O Lord my God, I pray thee, let this child's soul come into him again," Elijah said over and over.

Then the child began to breathe. He opened his eyes and seeing Elijah smiled at him. Elijah picked him up in his arms and carried him down the stairs into the room where the child's mother was sitting, weeping.

"See, thy son liveth," Elijah said as he stood the boy on his feet beside his mother.

When she saw her son standing beside her, strong and well, the widow woman looked up at Elijah and said reverently, "Now by this I know that thou art a man of God, and that the word of the Lord in thy mouth is truth."

from I KINGS, *chapter 17*

The Son of the Shunammite

*I*n Shunem there was a great woman who had everything to make her happy except a son.

Elisha in his journeyings often passed by the woman's house and she would invite him in to break his journey and eat with them. One day she told her husband that she was sure Elisha was a man of God and that it did honor to their house to have him stop by so often. This pleased her husband.

"Let us make a little chamber, I pray thee, on the wall. Let us set for him there a bed, and a table, and a stool, and a candlestick," she said to her husband. "And it shall be, when he cometh to us, that he shall turn in thither."

So they prepared a room for Elisha and it was always ready for him whenever he should be passing. This was such a convenience for Elisha that he wanted to do something in return for the Shunammite, so he asked his servant Gehazi what might be done to repay her kindness to him. Gehazi reminded him that the woman had no son.

"Call her," Elisha said.

When she stood before him in the doorway of the little room, he said to her, "About this time next year, thou shalt embrace a son."

She could not believe him, nor could she bear to have anyone make light of her dearest desire, so she said to him quickly, "Nay, my lord, thou man of God, do not lie unto thine handmaid."

But it happened as Elisha had said and in due time the woman bore a son. He was the joy of her heart and his father's pride and in all Shunem there were no happier people than the father and mother of the child whom the prophet had promised.

When the child had grown to be a boy, he went out one morning into the field where his father was working with the reapers. It was a cloudless day. The sun was pouring heat upon the land and there was no breeze to stir the trees. Because the work was so nearly done, the men were toiling hard and fast and the boy did his best to match his strength with theirs. Suddenly he dropped the armful of grain he was carrying and put his hand to his head.

"My head, my head," he said to his father.

The father put out his arms to catch his son so the boy would not fall on the rough stubble of the field. Then he said to a young man working nearby, "Carry him to his mother."

The child was carried home quickly and placed on his mother's lap. She held him to her, caressing him, talking to him, trying to waken him from the stupor into which he had fallen. But all her work was of no avail for by noon the boy was dead.

The Shunammite, still holding him in her arms, carried him to the little room she had prepared for the prophet. Placing the child on Elisha's bed, she went out and shut the door behind her.

Her husband had just returned from the fields to enquire after the boy, so she said to him, "Send me, I pray thee, one of the young men and one of the asses, that I may run to the man of God, and come again."

"Wherefore wilt thou go to him today?" he asked. "It is neither new moon, nor sabbath."

"It shall be well," she said.

Quickly she saddled the ass, saying to the servant who had brought it, "Drive, and go forward; slack not thy riding for me, except I bid thee."

So they went with all haste to

Mount Carmel where she knew the man of God was at that time.

Elisha saw her at a distance and turning to Gehazi said, "Behold, yonder is that Shunammite. Run now, I pray thee, to meet her, and say unto her, 'Is it well with thee? Is it well with thy husband? Is it well with the child?'"

Gehazi ran toward the woman and asked her the three questions Elisha had bade him, and to each one the woman replied, "It is well."

She did not pause in her journey but went on until she came to the hill where Elisha was standing. Then getting off her ass she knelt on the ground and put her arms around Elisha's feet. Gehazi tried to thrust her away.

"Let her alone," Elisha said, "for her soul is vexed within her. The Lord hath hid it from me, and hath not told me." He reached down and put his hand on the woman's head, comforting her in the hope that she would open her heart to him.

"Did I desire a son of my Lord? Did I not say, 'Do not deceive me?'"

The woman's words were muffled as she spoke for she kept her head bowed and she did not loose her hold on the feet of the man of God. Elisha knew that something terrible had happened to her son. Quickly he turned to Gehazi.

"Gird up thy loins," Elisha said, "and take my staff in thine hand, and go thy way. If thou meet any man, salute him not; and if any salute thee, answer him not again. And lay my staff upon the face of the child."

The Shunammite looked up into Elisha's face. "As the Lord liveth, and as thy soul liveth," she said, "I will not leave thee."

Elisha knew then that he would have to return with the woman to her home, for she would not be comforted until he had seen the child. So they followed Gehazi as he hastened on before them.

Gehazi went to the little room where the child was lying on the bed. Doing what his master had told him to do, he laid Elisha's staff across the face of the child, but many minutes passed and during them there was no sound from the child, nor any sign from him that he could hear the voice of Gehazi.

When Gehazi saw Elisha and the child's mother approaching in the distance, he went to them and said sorrowfully, "The child is not awaked."

Elisha made no reply and the woman kept her silence.

When they reached the house, Elisha went to the little room and there he saw the child, dead upon his bed. He shut the door behind him so that only he and the child were in the room. Then he prayed to the Lord.

After a few moments, he went to the bed and stretched himself upon the child so that his mouth was upon the boy's mouth, his eyes were upon the boy's eyes, and his hands covered the boy's hands that were so much smaller. The body of the child was cold and stiff, but after Elisha had lain upon him he could feel the flesh of the boy become warm, and the stiff limbs began to relax and assume natural positions. Elisha got up from the bed and walked back and forth across the floor of the small room, praying as he walked. After a while he stretched himself again across the body of the child, unceasing in his prayer.

Suddenly the child sneezed seven times, then opened his eyes as if someone had waked him from sleep and for a moment he did not know where he was. Seeing Elisha, whom he knew well, he greeted him cheerfully.

Elisha went to the door and spoke to Gehazi who was waiting outside. "Call this Shunammite," he said.

Gehazi went to fetch the mother of the child and when she came into Elisha's room he said to her simply, "Take up thy son."

Joy quickened her footsteps as she went toward her child, but before she reached the bed she dropped to her knees and bowed her head before Elisha. Then she went to the bed and put her arms around the little boy. She held him to her in a warm embrace while he twined his arms around her neck. Then she lifted him up and carrying the child in her arms went out of the room.

from II KINGS, *chapter 4*

The Little Serving Maid

At one time, when the armies of Syria were warring upon Israel, the Syrians returned to their camp with a little girl. She was hardly more than a child, but because she had been taken captive she was made a slave and waited on Naaman's wife. Naaman was a captain in the Syrian army. He was a great and honorable man in the eyes of the king of Syria, but he was a leper and the dread disease kept him apart from his fellows.

The little maid from Israel learned to do all that she should to serve her mistress, but she thought often of the land from which she had come and she longed for the day when she would be returned to her own people. She comforted herself by praying frequently and she was not unhappy, because the teaching in her home had been to trust the Lord in all ways. She knew that great good often came from what seemed like great misfortune and she reminded herself of the story of Joseph who had been sold as a slave into Egypt. It was a story her father had told her often and she remembered well the words Joseph had said when at last he was reunited with his brothers. "Be not grieved, nor angry with yourselves, that ye sold me hither," Joseph had said, "for God did send me before you to preserve life."

The little girl, comforting herself in this way, was far happier than the noble lady upon whom she waited. Naaman's wife was sad at heart because of her husband's illness and because there was no skill or power upon earth that could cure it. The Hebrew child knew that there was a prophet in her land that healed sick people and she longed to tell her mistress of Elisha. One day she did.

"I wish my lord were with the prophet that is in Samaria!" she said, "for he would cure him of his leprosy."

Naaman's wife was too full of her own sorrow to heed the words of her little slave and so she made no reply.

However, a servant standing near had heard. Leaving the room, he went to Naaman and told him what the child had said.

"Thus and thus said the maid that is of the land of Israel," he repeated, watching Naaman to see what he would do.

Naaman remained silent, but the king of Syria who valued the captain of his armies and felt willing to do anything to help restore him to health replied, "Go to, go, and I will send a letter to the king of Israel."

Naaman agreed to go, but he went with a great train bearing gifts—silver and gold and many changes of raiment. At the palace of the king of Israel, Naaman presented the letter from the king of Syria.

"Now when you receive this letter," the king of Israel read, "—the bearer is Naaman my servant—whom I have sent to you that you may cure him of his leprosy."

The king of Israel could not believe the words of the letter but thought that they must be a disguise for a quarrel the king of Syria was seeking, and he did not know what to do. But when Elisha heard that Naaman and his train had arrived at the Israelite court, he sent word to the king.

"Let him come now to me," Elisha said, "and he shall know that there is a prophet in Israel."

So Naaman went with his horses and chariot to the door of Elisha's house.

A servant came out to him with a message. "Go and wash in Jordan seven times, and thy flesh shall come again to thee, and thou shalt be cured."

That was not at all what Naaman had expected to hear and he went away angrily, saying to his serving men, "Behold, I thought, he will surely come out to me, and stand, and call on the name of the Lord his God, and strike his hand over the place and recover the leper. Are not Abana and Pharpar, rivers of Damascus, better than all the waters of Israel? May I not wash in them and be clean?"

"My father," one of his servants said as he approached him, "if the prophet had bid you do some great thing, would you not have done it? How much rather then, when he says to you, 'Wash, and be clean?'"

Naaman nodded his head as he saw the truth of what his servant said. Getting into his chariot, he went with all his train to the bank of the river Jordan. Then he left his men and went a little distance up the river.

Once and then twice he dipped himself into the waters of the Jordan, three times and then the fourth, while he kept his eyes lifted to the mountains of Israel and above them to Israel's God through whom healing came. Five times he lowered himself into the water and then the sixth. But at the seventh when he emerged from the water he saw that his flesh was restored like the flesh of a little child and that he was cured.

Then Naaman and all his company returned to the house of the man of God and this time Elisha stood in his doorway to greet him.

"Behold, now I know that there is no God in all the earth, but in Israel," Naaman said. "Now therefore, I pray thee, take a blessing of thy servant."

Elisha would take neither gold nor silver, no matter how Naaman urged it on him. "Go in peace," Elisha said, giving Naaman his blessing.

Naaman departed and went on his way back to Syria. During the journey he thought often of the little maid who had been so sure that if he would but see the prophet he would be healed.

from II KINGS, *chapter 5*

The Birth of Jesus

In the days of Caesar Augustus, a decree was made that all the people should be taxed, and for the taxing every man would have to go to his own city. Joseph lived in Nazareth but because he was a member of the house of David it was necessary for him to journey to Bethlehem. Mary, his wife, went with him. Joseph knew that Mary would soon have a child and he wanted to do everything for her comfort, so when they reached Bethlehem he went to the Inn and asked for a room. But the town was full of people and there was no room to be had at the Inn.

The best that Joseph could find for Mary was a stable near the Inn. They went there and after Joseph had made Mary comfortable and given the ass water and hay they settled down for the night. It was far quieter in the stable than in the Inn for the few animals that shared the small place with the visitors had already drooped their heads in sleep.

Toward midnight, Mary's child was born—a little son whom she called Jesus. She wrapped him in the swaddling clothes she had brought with her and laid him on the hay in the manger.

In the fields outside the town there were some shepherds who were watching over their flocks. Suddenly the darkness of the night around them was broken by light. They looked up and it seemed to them then as if the doors of heaven had opened before them, for the light and music that streamed from the

sky were so wonderful. The shepherds looked at each other in great fear. Then they heard an angel speaking to them.

"Fear not," the angel said, "for, behold, I bring you good tidings of great joy, which shall be to all people. For unto you is born this day in the city of David a Savior, which is Christ the Lord. And this shall be a sign unto you. Ye shall find the babe wrapped in swaddling clothes, lying in a manger."

The angel stopped speaking. But a great and glorious sound came from the open heaven. A multitude of angels were praising God and saying, "Glory to God in the highest, and on earth peace, good will toward men."

The sounds ceased and the light faded from the sky and the shepherds looked at each other.

"Let us now go even unto Bethlehem, and see this thing which is come to pass, which the Lord hath made known unto us."

"Let us go," they said one to another, as they folded their sheep and prepared to leave.

Throwing their cloaks over their shoulders and picking up their staffs, they hastened to the little town that lay just beyond the fields.

The angel had told them that they would find the babe lying in a manger and so the shepherds went with haste and without hesitation to the stable near the Inn. There they found Joseph and his wife Mary who had traveled so far that day. And there, just as the angel had said, was the baby who had been born to be a Savior.

They dropped to their knees to worship the child and then they repeated to Mary and Joseph what the angel had told them. Mary said nothing in reply, but she listened to their words and pondered them in her heart. Later on, when the shepherds went back to their sheep, they told all whom they met on the way of the wonderful things that had happened. And when they were alone again on the hillside they praised God for all that they had seen and heard.

The shepherds were not the only ones who came to bow before the child. Wise men came from the East, following the star which they had seen rise. First they went to Jerusalem.

"Where is he that is born King of the Jews?" they asked, "for we have seen his star in the East, and are come to worship him."

Herod, the king, was troubled at this for he wanted no king in Israel but himself. He called the wise men to him and asked them about the star. Then he sent them to Bethlehem saying, "Go and search diligently for the young child; and when ye have found him, bring me word again, that I may come and worship him also."

The wise men left the king and followed the star that went before them, and they did not stop until the star came to rest over the place where the child Jesus was. The wise men were filled with joy for they knew then that they had come to the end of their search.

Entering the house, they saw

the child with Mary, his mother, and they fell to their knees in worship of him. Then they opened their treasures and presented to him all that they had brought from so far, all that was of highest value—gold and frankincense and myrrh.

In spite of what Herod had asked of them, the wise men did not return to him for they knew that he intended no good for the child. When they left Bethlehem, they went by another way back to their own country.

One night, when Joseph was sleeping soundly, an angel came to him in a dream and said, "Arise, and take the young child and his mother, and flee into Egypt, and be thou there until I bring thee word, for Herod will seek the young child to destroy him."

Joseph arose and saddled the ass. Putting Mary on the ass with the child in her arms, they started by night on the journey into Egypt. Reaching there safely, they remained in Egypt until Herod was dead.

Again, while Joseph was sleeping, an angel came to him in a dream and said, "Arise, and take the young child and his mother, and go into the land of Israel, for they are dead which sought the young child's life."

So Mary and Joseph and the child Jesus returned to Israel, to the village of Nazareth where Jesus grew up.

from MATTHEW, *chapters 1 and 2 and* LUKE, *chapters 1 and 2*

The Boy Jesus

*E*very year Mary and Joseph journeyed from Nazareth to Jerusalem for the Festival of the Passover. Many of their friends and neighbors went too and the roads were busy with the people passing over them. Jesus used to like to accompany his parents on these journeys.

One day, when Jesus was twelve years old, they were on the way back to Nazareth after the Festival. Unknown to his mother and father, Jesus had remained behind in Jerusalem. Mary and Joseph were not aware of his absence for they thought he was somewhere in the company of people traveling over the road together. But when they had gone a day's journey and still Jesus had not joined them, they began to search for him among their relatives and friends.

They could not find him and there was no one who could remember having seen him since they had left Jerusalem. Finally, Mary and Joseph had to admit to themselves that Jesus must have been left behind in Jerusalem. So they hastened back as quickly as they could. Once they had reached the city they carried on their search for the twelve-year-old boy, but with no success.

It was not until the third day that they thought to go to the temple. There they saw Jesus sitting in the midst of the teachers, listening to them and asking them questions. But when the boy was asked questions, the learned men shook their heads in amazement at the intelligence he showed through the answers he gave them.

Mary and Joseph watching Jesus were so astounded that they could say nothing. Then Mary thrust her way through the circle of teachers and embraced her son. The sight of him after three days was a welcome one, and even reproof had to wait upon affection.

"Son," she said, "why hast thou thus dealt with us? Behold, thy father and I have sought thee sorrowing."

Jesus looked at her and in his quiet eyes was all the wisdom the older men had been seeking and the love he felt for all people. "How is it that ye sought me?" he asked. "Wist ye not that I must be about my Father's business?"

Neither Mary nor Joseph knew what he meant, but they were so happy to have found him again that they put all further questioning aside.

Jesus bade the teachers farewell and went with Mary and Joseph over the road to Nazareth. They traveled it alone this time for the company in which they had come were far ahead of them.

Jesus was obedient to his parents all the while that he was a boy growing to manhood in the quiet little town of Nazareth. He grew tall and strong and wise, gaining in favor both with God and with his fellow men. Often he said things that Mary did not understand, but she cherished his sayings in her heart.

from Luke, *chapter 2*

The Lad with the Loaves and Fishes

At one time when Jesus was healing and teaching in Galilee, he went down to the sea and crossed over to the other side. There was a hill on the far side of the lake and Jesus went there. The people thronged about him and no one wanted to leave his presence. Many of them were in need of healing and more were eager to listen to his teaching.

There were great numbers of people on the roads at that time journeying up to Jerusalem, for it was near the Feast of the Passover. Many of these people broke their journey for a while to join the crowds on the hillside who were listening to the Master. A young boy, walking along the road on his way to market with a basket of his mother's barley loaves and a few fish which he had caught in the lake, saw the crowds on the hillside and joined them. Because he was smaller than many of the others, and curious, he pushed his way easily through the crowd until he got up to the rim of people surrounding Jesus.

Andrew, one of the disciples, looked at the boy and moved over to make room for him. Seeing the boy's basket, Andrew said something to Simon Peter, his brother, who was standing beside him, and the two men nodded.

It grew to be late in the afternoon and Jesus began to feel concern for the people who had been with him all day and who now had nothing to eat. Turning to Philip, Jesus asked him in a low voice where bread could be bought that the people might eat. Philip shook his head and mentioning a large sum of money said that not even that would buy bread for so many people.

Andrew approached Jesus. "There is a lad here, who has five barley loaves, and two small fishes," he said. "But what are they among so many?"

All eyes turned on the boy and there was silence in the group surrounding Jesus. But among the people on the hillside there was eager talk and movement as they discussed among themselves those things the Master had been saying.

Jesus looked at the boy. Suddenly the lad realized that he who had been so insignificant was now the center of attention. He returned the Master's look and then, though no words passed between them, he left the edge of the crowd where he had been standing. He did not know what drew him. Of one thing only he was sure that he wanted to give to Jesus everything he had. Yet what he had seemed so little.

He approached the Master slowly and dropped to one knee before him. Then he held his basket forward and placed it at Jesus' feet. Poor as it was, it was all he had. There was silence in the group, so much so that a breeze ruffling the Sea of Galilee might have been heard in passing.

Jesus acknowledged the gift and the boy rose. Empty handed, he took his place again on the edge of the crowd.

"Make the men sit down," Jesus said.

Some of the disciples went out among the multitude telling the people to sit down. The words spread quickly from one group to another and soon all the people who had been standing on the hillside sat down on the grass. A great number they were, as many as five thousand. Even the circle of friends and disciples near Jesus sat down, and

the boy who had had the basket of loaves and fishes sat down in the grass as near to the Master as he could get. Soon there was only one figure standing on the green hillside.

Jesus reached down into the basket for one of the loaves. Then he looked up as people had seen him do so often when he would speak with his Father in heaven. The lad sitting near him did not hear him ask for anything, but he heard him give thanks for the good at hand.

Such a wave of gratitude for what was at hand spread through all the multitude of people that they did not remember their hunger.

Jesus then handed the five loaves to five of his disciples that stood near him. He told them to distribute the bread among the people that were sitting on the grass. The two fishes he picked up and gave to two disciples, asking them to do the same.

When the people had eaten enough to satisfy their hunger

and the disciples had returned to Jesus, Jesus said to them, "Gather up the fragments that remain, that nothing be lost."

So the disciples moved again among the people, each one with a basket, and when they returned it was to set down twelve baskets full of fragments of the five barley loaves and the two fishes which remained over and above all that they had eaten. Then a wondering murmur ran through the crowds on the hillside that had witnessed the miracle, and one man said to another, "This is truly the prophet that was promised to the world."

The boy's legs would not carry him fast enough as he raced down the hill, his empty basket light in his hand. He ran quickly over the road until he reached his own home.

"Mother, Mother," he cried, flinging the basket down.

She put her arms around him and welcomed him, but she did not ask him what he had received at market for the barley loaves she had given him to sell and the fishes he had caught. Swifter even than her son, someone else had come down the hill with the news of the mighty thing that had taken place—the news that a multitude of hungry people had been fed from so small a store. She could only be deeply happy that her son had been the one to help the Master and that their small supply had gone so far.

from JOHN, *chapter 6*

Jairus' Daughter

*I*n the house of Jairus, a ruler of the synagogue, there was great sorrow. Jairus' only daughter, a little girl about twelve years old, lay dying. Everything that could be done to help the child in her sickness had been done, but still she got no better. The mother of the little girl wept in sorrow and one by one her friends and neighbors came in to weep with her.

Then Jairus thought of Jesus, the teacher who was going about the country telling people of the Kingdom of God. And Jairus remembered that it had even been said of Jesus that he healed sick folk. Jairus hastened to find the teacher, but when he saw him he saw that a great crowd of people was surrounding him. However, Jairus pushed his way through the crowd and falling on his knees at Jesus' feet begged him to come to his house and help his child.

Before Jesus could answer Jairus, a man came running, thrusting his way through the crowd. Jairus recognized him as one of the servants of his household. The servant, seeing Jairus, approached him and bowed respectfully.

"Thy daughter is dead," he said. "Trouble not the Master."

Jairus could say nothing for a moment for the news filled him with sadness; but Jesus heard the servant's words and looking at Jairus he said, "Fear not: believe only, and she shall be made whole." Then he asked Jairus to lead the way to his house.

The crowd of people fell back, making an opening through

which Jesus could walk, followed by Peter and James and John. Jairus led the way, trying to still his sorrow with the challenge to believe that Jesus had given him.

When they reached the house, Jesus turned to the people standing outside and signalled to them that no one should enter the room where the little girl was lying except her father and mother and his faithful friends, Peter and James and John. But many people had already gathered in the room and all were crying and mourning as they stood near the child's bed.

Jesus looked at them and said, "Weep not; she is not dead but sleepeth."

Hearing his words the people began to laugh, but they laughed in scorn for they knew that she was dead.

Then Jesus told them all to leave the room; and because there was something in his tone that compelled obedience, they turned and filed slowly from the room. Not even the mother of the little girl who had been sobbing so piteously remained in the room. Not even the father who loved his daughter so dearly. Not even Peter or James or John who stood ready to do whatever Jesus might ask of them.

When they had all gone out and the last person had closed the door behind him, Jesus went over to the bed. He stood for a moment by the child who lay so white and still, her dark hair smooth on the pillow and her eyes closed. Then he reached down and took her hand in his. Calling to her as if she might have gone a small distance from him and needed to be brought back, he said, "Maid, arise."

Slowly her eyelids began to flutter and her eyes opened, a smile began to break across her lips as she saw Jesus standing beside her. Then she sat up. He put her hand down gently and went to the door to call her parents, but almost before they were in the room the child had leapt out of bed and run across the floor to them.

Jairus held his little daughter close to him, so happy he was to have her in his arms again, while the child's mother looked up at Jesus full of astonishment at what had happened.

"Give her something to eat," Jesus said quietly. Then calling to Peter and James and John he left the house of Jairus and went on his way.

from LUKE, *chapter 8*

The Child in the Midst

Jesus journeyed throughout Judaea telling people the good news of the Kingdom of God and telling them also what they must do to be worthy inheritors of it. His disciples—those twelve men whom he had chosen to carry on his teachings— went with him, sometimes all of them, more often just two or three. They talked about Jesus' teachings among themselves and often came to him with questions, eager for his answers.

One day, while they were in the vicinity of Capernaum, by the quiet waters of the Galilean Sea, the disciples approached Jesus. One, acting as spokesman for the others, voiced the question that had been troubling them.

"Who is the greatest in the kingdom of heaven?" he asked.

Jesus did not answer immediately. Looking around him, he caught sight of a child playing on the shore of the lake. Jesus called to him. The boy looked up from his game at the sound of the unfamiliar voice. Yet the voice had called him by his name as his mother or father might have done, so he dropped the pebbles with which he was playing and went to stand before Jesus.

"How can I serve you, sir?" he asked.

Jesus took him by the hand and drew him to a large rock near where he had been standing. The disciples grouped themselves around so that the Master and the child formed the center of a small gathering.

"Verily I say unto you," Jesus said, as he placed his hand on the boy's dark head and looked up at his disciples, "except ye be converted, and become as little children, ye shall not enter into the kingdom of heaven. Whosoever shall humble himself as this little child, the same is greatest in the kingdom of heaven. And who so shall receive one such little child in my name receiveth me."

The disciples nodded their heads and murmured together, for these were words they understood. Yet it was not the words alone but the presence of the child in their midst that made them realize the Master's teaching.

The child moved closer to Jesus and put his arm around the Master's neck, wanting to whisper something in his ear.

Jesus smiled at him as if to say that everything would come in good time. Looking across the boy's head and around the circle of men listening to him he said, "Take heed that ye despise not one of these little ones; for I say unto you, That in heaven their angels do always behold the face of my Father which is in heaven." Then he turned his attention to the boy.

The child, who had under-stood little of what Jesus had said to the men with him, knew what he wanted. He knew that he was in the presence of the Master and he had heard that the Master was a great story-teller. He even knew some of the stories that his parents had heard and told again in the lamp-lit evenings in the little house near which the waters of the lake lapped soothingly. Putting his lips close to the Master's ear, the small boy asked for a story.

Jesus smiled and talked direct-ly to the child, telling him about the man who had a hundred sheep. But, on a certain night when the sheep were brought back to their fold, he discovered that one was missing. He count-ed them a second time to make sure, but there were only ninety-nine. When he was satisfied that the other sheep were safe, he went back across the pasture land calling and looking; but no sheep did he find. Up into the hills he went, but no sheep came in answer to his call. And then further up the steep path into the mountains he climbed. There, high up in a place sur-rounded by rough crags, he found his sheep. The man reached down and comforted

the frightened, bewildered crea-
ture, then he lifted it up and carried it on his shoulders. So he
brought the wandering one back
safely to the fold.

Jesus looked at the small boy
and said, "The Son of man is
come to save that which is lost."

The boy put his hands together in his rapture at the tale, then
because he could not bear to
hear the kind low voice cease
speaking he asked to have the
story all over again.

Jesus laughed softly. "How

think ye?" he asked, putting his question to the boy. "If a man have a hundred sheep, and one of them be gone astray, doth he not leave the ninety and nine, and go into the mountains, and seek that which is gone astray? And if so be that he find it, verily I say unto you, he rejoiceth more of that sheep, than of the ninety and nine which went not astray."

The boy had been asked a question and he answered it solemnly as he moved his head up and down in agreement with all the Master had said.

Jesus was mindful of his wider circle of listeners. Looking up from the boy's face with its expression of eager, earnest lis-

tening, he spoke to his disciples.

"Even so it is not the will of your Father which is in heaven, that one of these little ones should perish."

The disciples had received their answer, they agreed among themselves; for in the kingdom of heaven there was no question of one being greater than another since all were equally beloved by the Father.

Soon Jesus and his disciples went on their way and the boy went back to his play, but as he built his toy village with pebbles on the shore of the lake he had a brave feeling. It was as real as the warmth of the sun at midday; as strong as his father's arms carrying him when he became tired. It was the knowledge that no matter what might happen to him, or where he might stray, it would never be too far for God to find him and bring him safely home.

from MATTHEW, *chapter 18*

*E*lizabeth Yates has written many books, and some of
them have been for children. Her children's book
Amos Fortune, Free Man was awarded the Newbery Medal
in 1951 and the first William Allen White Children's Book
Award in 1953. The Bible has always been a rich source of
inspiration for her, and in this small book she has taken spe-
cial delight in sharing the adventures of boys and girls who
live in the pages of the Bible with boys and girls living in
today's world. The words tell the stories, while the pictures,
with their careful detail, bring a faraway past into a happy
present; between words and pictures ranges imagination.